The End Of All Things

Poems of Love, Ruin, and Everything Between

Suyash Sisodia

BookLeaf Publishing

India | USA | UK

Made with ❤ on the BookLeaf Publishing Platform
www.bookleafpub.in
www.bookleafpub.com

Dedication

To the words that bled onto paper,
the ink that held me when no one else did,
the verses that kept me safe
when the world felt too loud, too quiet, too much.
You have been my refuge, my release,
my silent scream and my saving grace.
This is for you.

And to the lost, the searching, the healing—
this is for you, too.

Preface

Poetry has always been the language of everything we struggle to say aloud. It is love and loss, fire and silence, the weight of the world and the lightness of a moment. This book is all of that—it is everything I have ever felt, everything I have ever been.

I did not set out to write a collection of poems. I set out to survive. To make sense of the ache, to hold onto fleeting joy, to carve something lasting out of the impermanence of life. Somewhere along the way, these words became more than just mine. They became echoes of love, of heartbreak, of hope. They became a home for everyone who has ever felt too much.

This book is for the sad boy in class 8th who picked up a pen, not knowing it would change everything. It is for the late nights and lost days, for the songs that carried me, for the love that built me, and the heartbreaks that undid me. It is for the people who stayed and the ones who left, for the stories that ended and the ones still being written.

If you have ever felt like you are too much or not enough —these words are for you. If you have loved and lost, if you have burned and risen, if you have stood at the edge of everything and still chosen to go on—this book is for you.

This is not just a collection of poems. It is a testament to the fact that we survive. That we love, we break, and somehow, we find a way to begin again.

Welcome to The End of All Things.

Acknowledgements

To the ones who made this possible, in ways both big and small—thank you.

To my **parents** and my **brother** for being the quiet, unwavering pillars in the background of my story.

To the **beautiful thing called the internet**, where I found voices like mine, and voices unlike mine—both of which shaped me.

To the **sad boy in class 8th** who picked up a pen and didn't put it down—thank you for holding on, for believing, for writing even when it hurt.

To **A Wordsmith's Mind** and **The Bard Chronicles**, the communities I built, but which, in turn, built me. They were not just spaces; they were homes.

To **all the love** and to **all the heartbreaks**—you broke me, healed me, and, most importantly, made me write.

To **Reet, Stuti, and Sweekruti**, for keeping my sanity intact, sort of.

To **Aashna**, my best friend, my north star, my muse. For being the person I look up to, the one who reminds me why words matter.

To **Shravya**—I know you will never read this, but a lot of my words are because of you.

And to the **songs** that carried me through the storms, that whispered the words before I knew how to say them myself.

This book exists because of all of you. Thank you from every corner of my heart.

I.

I.

That's how it starts.
An I.

I, as in I want to get an icecream with you.
I, as in I like poetry
I like dogs,
I like old movies
and starwars.

I, as in I heard about this new place
I want to try it out,
I, as in I have this pet peeve
I don't like it at all.

It starts with I—
the nucleus of thought,
a whisper in the echo chamber of the self.

I, as in I saw the sky blush tonight,
painted in hues of secrets and half-forgotten dreams.
I, as in I felt the cold bite of the wind,
and it reminded me to breathe.

I, as in I like how your laughter feels
on the curve of your mouth,
I, as in I like the silence we keep,
comfortable and warm.

It starts with an I—
an amalgamation of life
thrown across a canvas blank.

I, as in I struggle to keep the demons at bay,
that haunt me night and day
I, as in I live on borrowed smiles
that seem to be collecting their debt.

I, as in I am collecting pieces of myself
like seashells on this seashore,
scattered and spread,
but all mine to hold.

I, as in I heard a song today
and it reminded me of you,
soft, composed, and calm,

all things you are for me.

It starts with an I—
filled with desires
filled with tries.

I, as in I want to explore Greece
with you at my side.
I, as in I am okay with your baggage
as long as you are with mine.

I, as in, I am yours
and you are mine
and all these scars
and all these lines
shall tell a story of you and mine.

I, as in I do,
in sickness and in health,
to love and cherish,
till its you and I,
till death do us apart.

It starts with I,
but it doesn't end there.
I becomes we,
in the tender collision of voices and truths,

in the merging of edges and shadows.

It begins with I—
a singular, solitary star—
but oh, how constellations are born.

Tick Tock

Tick-Tock Tick-Tock
round goes the clock,
a toothbrush, two similar shirts
and a tie to round it all.

Day 1:

I wake up with the alarm;
the alarm dies down,
and I hear my own heartbeat
all alone in this 4 by 4 room.

I wake up. I rise.
Rinse. Spit. Repeat.

I put on a shirt,
and the matching tie,
and leave again,
no one to say goodbye.

Day 2:

I wake up before the alarm,
the nightmares haunt me still.
I freshen up and step out,
I follow my routine.

Rinse. Spit. Repeat.

The ground lays empty
but for one shadow in the dark.
Who comes so early
to the park?

Day 3:

Rinse. Spit. Repeat.

I couldn't sleep tonight,
So I just go to the park.
Before the sun could rise
or dogs could bark.

I see the figure again,
it's a she,
Oh no, she's coming
to me.

What?
Why?
How?
No. No. No.
Just a mistake,
I'm sure of it all.

"Hello," she speaks,
Her face becomes clear.
Panic. Alarm. Crisis.
I disappear.

Day 4:

"Hello,"
It rings in my mind
a greeting soft,
a greeting kind.
Questions. Panic.
More questions arise.

I look at my 4 by 4,
and I rise.

Rinse. Spit. Repeat.
I hurry to the park,

before the sun comes up
or the dogs bark.

I see her again,
a shadow standing tall,
and panic rises again,
Like I would fall.

Stupid Stupid!
that's all I think,
and suddenly she appears
and I swear I couldn't even blink.

What?
Why?
How?
I question it too.
But she asks my name,
and I let it all go.

Seconds. Minutes. Hours.
We talk about her tale,
and I listen to every word
I listen without fail.

Day 5:

Scents. Colours. Songs.
Everything feels so bright.
I wake up next to her,
and it just feels right.

Rinse. Spit. Repeat.

Heartbreak. Pain. Loss.
Fear cowers mind.
Day 6, Day 7, Day 8, Day 9,
all pass and she is still mine.

Day 10:

We go shopping
my room is filled with art
there's colours now too,
and a little heart.
We buy me a new wardrobe,
"I want to style you too,"
and with her I'm sure,
I'm born anew.

Rinse. Spit. Rise.

There's more to my life.
A paintbrush and pastel tones,

we paint my room alive
Oh! I think I'm falling for her,
but how deep can I dive?

Days passed, weeks turned over,
and soon a year,
and ever since we met,
I have had no fear.

Day 365:

She lies sick
as I sit by her side,
And tears roll down
that I cannot hide.
The doctors tell me
she has a month
and after that the dark,
but how is that even possible?
We just met in the park.

Rinse. Spit. Repeat.

How is it fair?
She's the one sick,

and I'm gasping for air.

Rinse. Spit. Repeat.

The routine goes on.
She's here now,
soon she'll be gone.
She whispers sickly,
"My life, my love,
do not worry,
look above.
The stars shine,
our love will too,
I wish I could stay,
but now you do for two."

Day 395:

I wake up with the alarm;
the alarm dies down,
and I hear my own heartbeat
all alone in this 4 by 4 room.

I wake up. I rise.
Rinse. Spit. Repeat.

I put on a shirt,
and the matching tie,
and leave again,
looking at the sky.

I go out to the park
and watch the sunrise,
I look at the kids play with the dogs,
I watch the flowers shine.

She is gone
and that is true
but ever since I met her
my life became less blue.
She used to say,
"Life is short
and there's so much to do,
so never stop living
no matter what you do."
So I come here every day
to this beautiful park,
for who knows what adventures
I might find, after the dark.

April to my life

I was the month of September,
and you were the April to my life,
and we made love in the winter,
when all the world was frozen tight.

They told me of the winter horrors,
of how the heart freezes shut,
they told me of the worlds broken
by the winter's grudge.

I used to believe in their stories,
in their half-webbed lies,
till I saw you on that fateful evening,
and the winters were made alive.

The white of the winter,
a peaceful sign,
and the deadening trees,
just waiting to come to life.
Winters were not horror,

they were the blossom of life,
and what can begin that doesn't end,
in this circle of life.

So when I say I was the month of September
and you were the April to my life,
I tell all that winters can blossom
even the souls that seem to be dying.

So when I say I was the month of September
and you were the April to my life,
I mean you are my muse,
the love of my life.

Dial the Clock Back To You

I wish to sit in front of a clock,
turn its dials back to you—
to warmth and emotions,
to cuddles and life.

I have lived that moment
again, and again, and again,
where I held your hand,
and yours held an ice cream.
And oh, how I was happy.

"You're. Killing. Me."
Words spoken in a moment of affection,
a moment of us.
the time when I knew you'd be here.
You made me promise
you made me say,
you made me believe you
that I'll stay.

I remember you doting on me,
your patience,
your kindness,
the way you cared
even when I didn't deserve it.

I did love you, you know?
I did.
I want you to know—
I did.

But I was hurting.
And I never had time—
for your laughter,
your hugs,
your needs.

I was selfish.
I was blind.
And one day,
I looked up—
and I was alone.

You called yourself a potato—
lazy, cute,
soft against the world.
You went with everything—

hoodies, tees,
and even me.

But you left.
Because you had enough.

I still read the letters,
the ones that made my birthday special.
Yet, I hurt you.
Even though I cared.

Can I drop to my knees
and ask for forgiveness?
Can I drop everything
and hope you come by.
I'm forgetting your voice now,
and with time,
maybe your face will fade too.
but I'll never forget how warm I felt with you
and how barren it has been since I lost you.

You've moved on
to a life of your own,
with people you deserve
and happiness you need.
so yes, I wish to sit in front of a clock
and turn its dial back to you.

But maybe I won't
for you are better off without me,
so I'll just sit in a corner
and wish you luck from afar.
May letting you go
be my final kindness.

All you do is watch

There's no water in my lungs
yet I am drowning still,
I'm in a landslide of emotions
rolling down the hill.
I need a voice,
or a hug,
or a hand,
or a soul,
to just...
give me a reason,
to give me some hope.

Even with so many people,
and over 400 contacts in my phone
I feel broken and crushed,
I feel so alone.

I...
don't have words,
to describe this feeling,

of anguish, of hurt,
and not of healing;
It feels like a gentle breeze at first,
then an annoying sound of a fly,
but tonight,
I feel it in my heart,
in my bones,
in every bit
of what my existence
could hold.

Hear me, someone.
Please.
Help me out.
I see laughter
and life,
I see people
and their smile.
I see happy faces
and beating hearts
and I can't help but wonder—
How do people do that,
be happy?

My eyes are dry
my heart bleeds out,
onto people

and paper
and all that I can hold;
and I hope—
to be heard,
to be helped
to be taken away.
It's dark here
and I cannot breathe,
I'm dying a slow death,
and no one can even see.

I'm crying,
I seek help,
please come to me,
please hear my welp.
I'm screaming my lungs
can you not hear?
Can you not see me
broken and in fear?

Or can you see?

Can you see all this
and choose to look away?
Choose to turn away an eye
because it's easier that way.

Do you put earplugs
to drown my screaming
and put on an eye mask
to not see me breaking?
Is it as easy as plucking
a flower from a garden
or does conscience
make it a bit harder
to see me fading?

Does it even matter?
Do my words even reach you?
It's hard being a poet, you know
not just because you feel more
but because your words
are emotions to you,
but for them they are just...
art.
Everyone loves it,
but few ever wonder
about the pain and tragedy
behind that craft.

Do you?
Do you see my pain?
Or like everyone else
you find the beauty

in my pain,
the love
in my heartbreak.
I'm breaking,
I'm broken,
I sinking,
I am sunken,
no water in my lungs,
yet I drown,
and all you do
is watch.

The Heartbreak that breathes

All my life
I used to think that heartbreaks are silent,
a moment when the world
would fold in on itself,
swallowing the noise,
the colours,
the life.

All poems I consumed
or movies watched
music heard
or conversations had
all said the same -
that heartbreaks are silent,
a stopping of all things.

Yet,
now I know they were all
wrong.

It isn't silent,
it's loud and breathing,
a living thing that grows in the hollow spaces.
It consumes the air,
fills my chest with its weight,
and yet leaves me empty.

It grows,
not like a fire that devours,
no.
It grows like roots,
a little each day,
till all there exists are the roots
wrapped around your broken heart,
sinking deep,
binding me to the pain
that birthed it in the first place.

You can try to drown it,
in the noise of the city
of songs
of movies,
but it doesn't silence heartbreak,
no.
It's always there waiting,
always there breathing.

Heartbreak,
it's like a pulse,
a constant rhythm of living reminder
that tell you with every breath,
all the loss
you ever faced.

And in the quiet hours of the night,
when the world forgets to spin,
I feel it most—
its breath,
its weight,
its unbearable, endless presence.

So no,
heartbreak is not silent -
a stopping of all things,
Heartbreak is loud
breathing
creeping
devouring
till all that remains
is a husk of what was once
and you lie there thinking -
will it ever stop breathing?

The Paper Ring

I don't suppose people tell you about this,
and I don't blame them,
for this silence is too loud to be put in words,
too muted to be heard.
It's suffocating,
like the dreams of Friday the 13th,
both horrifying and deadly,
and yet—somehow—unreal.

This feels unreal.

The house is quieter without you,
not just in sound but in the way the air settles,
as if even the walls know you are gone.
The coffee machine hums,
but no one argues over how strong it should be.
The faucet drips,
but there is no laughter between the drops.

The wind nudges the curtains, but they do not dance—

they only shift, restless, waiting.
I pass the couch we swore would last forever,
the cushions still holding the shape of us.
The TV hums in the background,
last night's show looping in an empty room,
laugh tracks bouncing off the walls,
but no one's laughing now.

Your mug sits on the table,
red lipstick smudged on the rim,
a quiet signature,
a reminder that you were here.
Isn't it the same one?
The one from the fair,
the one I got you,
the one you wouldn't let go of,
the one that made you say, "*See?
We just fit.*"

I trace the edge with my thumb,
like touching it might bring you back,
like love could still be poured into it,
like some things aren't already gone.
Didn't you promise me a forever?
Didn't you say you'd stay?

I remember it was New Year's Eve,

and like any couple who had stopped counting
anniversaries,
we were in our jammies,
curled up against the fire.
The glow of it danced across your face,
soft and golden,
but nothing shone brighter than the way you looked at
me.
Your hand found mine,
fingers warm, fingers sure,
and then—
a ring.

Not gold, not silver,
just the twisted remains of a candy wrapper,
delicate, weightless, but somehow,
heavier than diamonds.
You slipped it onto my finger
pressed a kiss against my cheek,
soft as the whisper that followed.
"Oh honey," you said,
"you know what this means?"
"This means you are stuck with me forever,
till we are old and grey."
But the fire burned down,
and the years folded away.

And now—
Now, the house is quiet,
holding the memories and me and you>
Your keys are still by the counter,
Your shoes sprawled across the floor.
Your coat is hung on the chair,
waiting to be worn by you,
and this room... oh, it smells just like you.
Like your shampoo,
like your perfume clinging to the air,
like something soft, something safe,
something that shouldn't be gone.
But as I look down,
my shirt—
still stained with you.
Dark brown now, but I know what it was,
what it is.
The same colour I watched pool beneath you,
watched soak into my hands as I begged,
"Stay with me."
"Please, stay."

A bullet,
not meant for you,
just a stray,
came and undid you.

Just like that.

No warning, no grand goodbye,
just the sharp gasp of your breath,
just the weight of you collapsing into me,
just the way your fingers curled into my sleeve,
like you were holding on,
or maybe—maybe trying to let go.
The EMTs told me to change
but I couldn't,
I couldn't scrub it away,
I couldn't let you go.
So the shirt clings to me now,
like a second skin,
like you,
the last proof that you were here,
the last I will ever have of you.

So now the coffee machine hums,
and the faucet still drips,
the wall still stands,
and the clock still ticks,
like they don't know the house is missing you.
Like they don't know I am, too.
So your mug is still on the table,
your lipstick still on the rim,
and I trace the edge with my thumb,

Didn't you promise me forever?
Didn't you say you'd stay?
The ring sits in a drawer, crumpled but unbroken.

Unlike you.

Unlike me.

Too Far Gone

I was told that
time can heal all the pain,
that there is a rainbow
after there is rain.

They told me that
all our scars fade,
that pain is not permanent,
that there is a way.

They told me that time has the power
to fix all my mistakes
to fix all the errors
and mend all the cracks and breaks.

They told me time is the cure.
They told me like they are sure.

Does it though?
Does time make it better

or is it just a fairy tale
wrapped in glitter paper?

\—

I am gone
bring me back,
shine some light
through the crack,
Was it hope
that just left?
Am I alone
in this mess?

\—

I have been standing here,
watching butterflies tear through the air
like they own the sky,
Like they know no fear.
And I wonder—
do they ever hear the discordant cries trapped inside my
heart?
Do they ever pause mid-flight,
and wonder why I am still standing here,
why I am watching my world collapse into embers
but never moving, never flying,
never reaching for the wind?
Do they see me?
Do they know?
I have been standing here,

watching my world burn,
and the ashes of my dreams
smother me until I can't breathe,
until I run.

But I'm tired now.
Tired of running away.
I've been running for years,
running from my own skin,
running from my own fears.
But all I can hear now are echoes—
empty futures and broken hearts,
and no time can mend them,
no hand can take me that far.

—
I am in pain,
help me out,
let it rain,
get me out.
I am weak,
don't let me break,
I can't swim,
don't let me drown.
—

Do you now know
the stories I've told,
or do I still need to say more?

I am crushed beneath the weight
of all I've bored,
all I've kept hidden,
all I've endured.
I have walked your paths,
I have reached for your hand,
but nothing—
nothing can pull me
out of this quicksand.

—

I'm broken,
I'm dead,
I'm all that's never said.
I'm the voice unheard,
I'm the ashes unburnt,
I'm lost,
I'm scared,
I'm broken,
but nobody even cares.

—

I wander through the darkness I roam,
Too far I've strayed, too far from home.
No path remains to guide me back,
No trail to lead me from this track.

—

I am crying,
wipe my tears,

stand by me,
to face my fears,
I am afraid
of being alone,
to have no one cry
at my stone.

Look at me,
I am here,
I need your support,
more than ever.
My mind is broken,
my soul is hurt,
but maybe you can help me,
clean out some of the dirt.

Run.
I am here.
Look at me.
Show some care.
I need love.
I can fight.
I can live.
I can survive.
No!
Don't go.
I am here.

So when I bid you
A farewell and a goodbye,
know it's for the last time.
I am tired of everything
tired of life.
I can't run anymore,
I can't fight anymore,
I can't just stand here
and keep going.
Darling,
not anymore.

Losing of a friend

It's muted chaos,
losing of a friend.
Underrated.
Underfelt.

It isn't grand,
like loss of love
or life
or even property.
It's concealed,
hidden in the silent cries,
hidden in forgotten memories
and inside jokes that died.

Like that question—
"If a tree falls in a forest
and no one is around to hear it,
does it make a sound?"
I ask,
If a laugh was shared

between two people
and one is gone,
was it ever really laughed?

I have lost so many,
I no longer keep count.
To time,
to space,
to silence,
to my own undoing.
And it is never just them—
if it were,
that would be mercy.

No.

When you lose people,
you lose pieces of yourself,
the ones that only existed in their presence,
the versions of you
that lived in their laughter,
in their knowing glances,
in the words you only ever spoke
when they were there to listen.

In friendship,
you create worlds,

and stories strung together
like constellations in the sky,
there's language you own,
and jokes you share,
and that is just with them.

And I mourn alone to their death,
for who will understand my pain,
other than the one who left?

There was this girl,
Summer of 20' we met,
and she was sweet and kind,
and beautiful and wise,
and she was my friend,
and then she wasn't.

And I mourn,
not for a life lost,
but for the echo of a bond undone,
for the death of a person still breathing—
same face, same name,
but different.

Nobody talks about this pain—
not the grand, cinematic grief,
not the kind that drowns you in tears,

but the quiet ache,
the slight pause before the punchline
that will never land.
The pain of finding that one joke,
that specific kind of stupid,
the kind only you and them
would laugh at.
And for a moment,
your fingers twitch,
your mind reaches—
you almost send it.
But then you remember.
And the joke,
once bright and full of air,
falls flat in the silence.
Nobody talks about the way grief hides
in laughter that never gets shared.

Tell me,
what do I do with this muted chaos,
this ache that never dies?

What do I do
with the pieces of myself
scattered like leaves
gone before their time?

What do I do with this knife,
gut-wrenching, twisting,
every time I remember
what is no longer mine?

I am a walking graveyard,
of half-forgotten moments,
of stories that never found their ending,
of everything else that died.

And I mourn alone,
in the quiet between heartbeats,
for the friendship that isn't,
for the parts of me
that will never see the light.

To belong

I wish you don't feel these words,
the ones I am about to pen down.
I wish your world is softer,
your weight is lighter,
that life is kinder to you.

It wasn't for me.

The thing is,
when you are like me—
loud, bright,
the one who fills a room with laughter,
the one who always has the right words,
the one they call
smart,
funny,
popular—
They assume you are okay.
That you have people.
That you could never be alone.

But that isn't true.

I don't think people realise
how a crowded room can feel like a void,
how laughter can taste bitter,
when there's no one to share it with,
how being known by people,
or being surrounded by them,
doesn't equate to being *seen*.

and maybe—
that's the worst kind of loneliness,
the one that no one believes.

Most of my life,
I have felt like I am living
behind a one-way glass.
Here,
existing,
breathing,
but unheard,
unseen.
I watch,
I listen,
I laugh on cue,
but the sound never reaches them.

Muted laughter—
a group, a circle, a world
that I stand beside,
never within.
I do not belong,
not really,
not in the way that matters.
They never see me—
not the way I need to be seen.

Do you know how it feels
to not belong?
To not be seen?
To walk into rooms that know you
but never make space for you?
To scream so loud
that your throat hurts
and your lungs burn
and be unheard still?

I hope you don't,
I hope the world is softer for you,
more open,
and you are heard,
and seen,
and embraced.

But I do.
I know it too well.

Maybe I am the problem,
maybe it is all me.

Maybe it's the way my thoughts unravel,
or how I exist in spaces not built for me.
Maybe it's my voice,
too sharp,
maybe too low,
or just not the right frequency.
Or maybe it's my ideas,
my thoughts that stretch beyond what follows.

Or maybe it's—
I don't know,
I really don't.

All I do know is this ache,
this want to belong,
to be heard,
to be held,
to be seen.

All I know is this ache,
of being too much,

and never enough,
at the same time.

48

Words don't come as easy

Words don't come to me as easy as they used to.
I was full of them once—
Words I mean.
They flew through me like I was some
open window,
no need for summoning, no pause for thought.

But now they hesitate,
like birds unsure of the sky,
perching by the edges of my pen,
fluttering,
then retreating.

I always believed no matter how bad it gets,
I'll have my words,
that my poetry will carry me through
even when life itself seems to refuse,
but lately?
Lately, I've been feeling like a page left blank,
a stanza unfinished,

a thought cut short before it finds its voice.

Lately, the pages are heavier,
the ink, dry,
and I just can't seem to do again
what I've done all my life.
Write.
It's like my words have grown tired of me,
or I, of them,
and now all that is left
is an abandoned graveyard
of...
something,
something I could write about once,
but not anymore.

I trace old verses with trembling hands,
wondering if they still belong to me,
if they ever did.
I once believed poetry would catch me
when everything else let go—
but what happens when even poetry stumbles?
When the muse turns silent,
and the echoes fade?

What does a poet do without his words,
without the very thing that makes he?

Stripped of his bare,
and hollowed out of verses
what remains
but the echoes of what used to be
him?

Does he search the silence,
dig through the dust of forgotten lines,
beg the wind to carry back
what once came so freely?
Or does he learn to live without them,
to exist as something lesser,
a poet in name only—
a vessel emptied of song?

Maybe that's why I am here
As I press my pen to paper,
waiting, hoping,
that the words will come to me
like they used to.

Today I laugh at your hollow promises

Today I laugh at your hollow promises
those empty words of love.
soft syllables of you and I,
woven into the fragile hope of us.

I once believed in the way you smiled at me,
believed that behind your gaze lay something real,
but now, those smiles are ghosts,
memories turned to dust,
whispers in the silence of my empty hands.

The love that never was,
is that all that I ever lost?
Or did I lose the dream we spun,
stitched together with shared moments,
with stolen glances, midnight confessions,
and quiet laughter in the spaces between our words?
A dream that became a paradise,
where once stood out castle of love.

only to crumble beneath the weight of time,
of truth,
of you.

Do I blame you?
Do I?
Can I?

You told me you are fickle,
I loved you still,
You told me I am not to be trusted,
I loved you still.
Perhaps I loved the idea of us
more than I ever loved the truth.
Perhaps I was blind—

Blind to the pain.
Blind to the way you wounded me
with words unsaid,
with promises broken,
with the needs unfulfilled.
Blind to the truth
of you.
Blind to how abusive you were
to me and you.

But tell me—

what did I do to deserve this?
To deserve the lies,
the empty echoes of your affection,
the way you kissed another
and told me you liked it.
As if my heart was not already breaking.
As if my love was not already bleeding.
As if I was nothing more than a casualty
of your restless, wandering heart.

And so—
today I laugh at your hollow promises
those empty words of love,
smiles you shared with me,
memories turned to dust.
Not crying,
not laughing,
just starting at the ruins of what could have been,
waiting for the day I no longer ache
for the love that never was.

The End?

...and then it fell,
slowly,
gradually,
then all at once—

like the last leaf surrendering to autumn's hush,
like the final thread snapping in a tapestry too worn to
mend,
like the last whispered I love you
spoken into the silence of an empty room.

Usually,
it ends here—
the words softened with time,
woven into stories meant for remembering,
carved into poetry,
scribbled on the last pages
of an old, forgotten notebook.

But what comes next?

What happens to me
when your name no longer lingers on my lips,
when the echo of your laughter dissolves into the hush
of passing days,
when even the sun, golden and endless,
fails to remind me of your warmth,
your presence,
your touch?

There's no TV shows on that
telling me what to do,
or books of post-romance
that I relate to.

No.

It starts as a gentle breeze first,
a strange sensation in you,
a feeling of weightlessness,
a feeling of you.
and then—
there's space.
Not a void,
not an absence of you,
just an empty space that has nothing to do with you,
something that breathes in places

where you once lingered.

Like the end,
it doesn't happen all at once.
No grand revelation,
no cosmic signs,
just a shift,
a whisper,
a feeling of you going away,
from what is I.

At first,
it's the way how the silences don't scream your name,
or how your favourite ice cream no longer tastes bitter.
Then,
it's the flowers.
Daisies,
that you always had my side,
spilling over me, and I,
smile, just no longer thinking of you.

Eventually,
it's the laughter—
my own,
unspooled from me
without the weight of echoes.

No books prepare you for this,
no TV show scripts it cleanly,
but here I am,
standing at the edge of something unnamed,
no longer tethered to yesterday.

Not the end.
Not quite.
Just a beginning,
wearing the quiet disguise of nothing at all.

the end days

#Poetry I wrote for her at the end days.

It was a lifetime,
the story of you and me.
So much has come,
so much has gone,
but one moment stays—
clinging,
refusing to fade.

It loops in my mind,
like a song caught in a broken tape,
spinning,
playing,
again,
and again,
and again,
as if time itself were stuck.

T'was a summer day,

a sunny Wednesday in June,
the sun high,
scorching,
melting,
bright,
pushing us all indoors.

I remember because I was at Joe's Cafe,
morning paper in hand.
T'was a tardy day,
and boring news,
something about politics,
something death,
and so it would have remained,
if I hadn't seen you.

I looked up from the pages,
and you stood there tall,
and Gods, you took me by surprise,
a storm.
YOu were kneeling over the crossword puzzle,
a pencil roaming in your hand,
and oh,
as if the world outside had never existed,
as if it was just you and those black-and-white squares.

I had seen you before,

it's not like it was the first time.
You'd always be trodding to the market,
or hopping about town,
or going to that Cafe on Second Street with friends,
or hanging around on your own.

But that day,
but that morning—
that was the first time I looked at you.

God be my witness,
you were beautiful.
Not in the way the world defines it,
not in the way light catches skin or silk drapes a frame,
but in the way you felt—
a quiet, impossible force
that made me forget how to stop smiling.

I saw my past, present, and future in you,
I saw my wife,
I saw the mother of my child,
I saw everything in you.

I don't know if it was love,
or just adrenaline surging through my veins,
but the world hushed,
the noise drained,

and for the first time in a long time,
there was only you.

I know you know this story,
and every time I tell you,
you say I am exaggerating,
that poets make a living on hyperbole,
but I swear—
that's exactly how it was.
That's exactly how you made me feel.
That's exactly how I have felt with you,
how I feel with you,
all along.

Of course, I didn't walk up to you that day.
It took me days, weeks—
stalking, convincing—
before you agreed to go out with me.

But I remember the morning I first saw you.
It was the summer of '86.
And you smelled of peaches and strawberries.

The Hollow of Being

I am,
and yet I am not.
A shadow, a smudge,
a breath caught in a throat
that never learned how to exhale.

The weight of existence
is heavier than death's promise,
pressing bones into the earth
before they are ready to lie still.
Each heartbeat
feels borrowed,
each thought
an unwelcome guest.

What is life,
but the endless unravelling
of a thread too thin to hold?
A spiral of whispers,
a cacophony of echoes

that never find their source.

Pain lives in the marrow.
It sings its discordant hymn
through veins that ache to be emptied.
Loss is a house
without doors or windows,
a place you never leave
but can never call home.

Sometimes, I wonder
if the sky mourns
the stars it devours.
If the earth regrets
swallowing the bodies
it once nurtured.

I hold myself in fragments,
shattered glass
cutting the hands that try to heal.
There is beauty in breaking,
they say.
But they do not tell you
how it feels to fall.

To exist
is to drown in silence.

To not exist
is to crave the noise.
Somewhere in between,
I hover.
Neither alive nor dead,
just
a whisper.

Who am I?

Life is a bittersweet circle,
with no beginning in sight,
it's just one dream after another,
does that even seem right?
It has been a while since I've had this talk,
of sharing who I am and not of the path I walk.

I am **blacked-out**
can you see me still?
would you attempt to know me
do you have the will?
I'm a happy face in the crowd, a smile of whom everyone
is proud,
but inside,
I'm broken
I'm dead
I'm all
that's never said.

I'm the voice unheard,

I'm the ashes unburnt,
I'm lost,
I'm scared,
I'm broken,
and nobody even cares.

My life is a one-way glass
where I see people and feel their echoes ring
yet I am invisible and unheard,
uncertain and undone.
I wish I knew who I am,
a son,
a brother,
a friend,
a lover,
or am I just a blurring memory of a distant past,
a has-been who didn't last.
I sense I am lost
and my identity in shambles,
I put it together like a house of cards,
but one gust,
and it comes crumbling down.

I wish to be broken verses and free lines,
I wish to be me, just undefined.
but I'm words on a document,
Times New Roman, 12, Justified,

living my life within the norms confined.

I do it to be accepted,
to be mattered,
to be seen,
to be heard,
and yet I'm backspace
when I'm no longer of use.
is that all that is,
is life one big ruse?
I feel broken today
however, hope lingers on,
of the long road ahead,
of time and its promises,
of dreams yet to come.

Life is a bittersweet circle,
with no end in sight,
it's just one dream after another,
that's what makes it right.

If you stop loving me

I once asked you—
if you ever stop loving me,
will you be brave enough to let me know?

I thought we were ending.
I thought my life had collapsed,
but then you came to me,
held my hand,
said you loved me,
that nothing would break us,
and I smiled.

My love for you was true.
I believe yours was, too.
But tonight,
I sit alone,
ink-stained hands trembling over paper,
heart wrenching music filling the silence,
thinking of you—
and I smile.

I was happier with you,
better with you.
And though you deny our past,
my heart remembers.
Somewhere deep down,
I know you do too,
somewhere deep down,
you feel it—
and I smile.

Now, I am just a name,
someone you once knew.
But to me,
you have always been the same,
and I will always love you.
Your heart belongs to another now.
I knew it the moment you gave it away,
because mine ripped apart.
And still,
I smile.

You are happy,
far away from me,
in the arms of someone new.
And I smile,
watching you,

because maybe one day I will love again,
but you—
you will always be my first.
The one I loved in innocence,
the one I will look back on,
the one who taught me,
who shaped me,
who made me.
You will always be the one.

And maybe—
someday, years from now,
I will call you up,
and we will talk
like we did the first time.
Because, my love,
you are the one
I am never letting go.

She Says She Doesn't Love Me

I used to be a blot of existence,
adrift in an undying universe—
a void of unforgiving solitude,
where time blurred,
where now and tomorrow bled together
like an open wound,
draining whatever I had left of life—
or whatever my existence was called.

Then I saw colours.
Red, yellow, blue, green—
they spilt into my monochrome,
spreading across my emptiness,
blending into something new,
something alive.
They were the colours of hope,
of friendship, of stability,
of love.
They were **her** colours.

And she painted them across my life.

Like a dwindling flame
on a winter's night,
I was on the brink of collapse—
then she walked in,
carrying fire in her hands,
burning brighter than the stars.
She made me alive.
She made me happy.
She gave me a reason to survive.
Her hands,
gentle warmth against the cold,
a comfort when everything else
was falling apart.

In her eyes,
I found myself.
For a moment,
the world washed clean,
soft as the hush before dawn.
She carries the soul of a child,
the heart of someone who loves
more than she knows,
more than she will ever admit.
She tells me she doesn't believe in love,
that she doesn't love me.

But I have seen it—
the flicker in her gaze,
the quiet tremble of something
too deep to name.
She can say it,
deny it,
pretend love is a stranger
she will never welcome home.

But love—
it does not ask permission.
It seeps through cracks,
finds the smallest space,
and stays.

So when I close my eyes tonight,
I will not fear the dark,
will not shrink from the silence.
Love has found me now,
and it is here to stay.

I think I'm falling

Entry 1: 10/06/2020

I think I'm falling—
not just into love,
but into the way she speaks,
the way she listens,
the way she tucks her hair behind her ear
like it's the most natural thing.
It's been so little time,
and yet my heart spills over.
If I am the One,
then,
she is The Other One,
tying our hearts together
with words and the hope of tomorrow.

Entry 2: 12/06/2020

My heart is full, it overflows,
My mouth is dry, lost in endless smiles.

She wears her heart, so soft it shows,
on the sleeves of her kindness.

She makes the time, she makes the space,
She builds a world where I belong.
With every glance, with every trace,
She turns my silence into song.

I think I want to make her mine,
To hold her close and stop the time..
I think I want to make her mine—
for her, I'd even make this free verse rhyme.

Entry 3: 17/08/2020

Oh, she's here! She's here!
Ssssh—
The Other One to my One,
The rhyme to my free verse,
the remover of pain,
the bringer of joy.
Oh, my love,
my love,
my love,
you're forever mine.

Entry 4: 18/09/2020

It's my birthday
and she's here,
and if I say I need no gifts
for all I need is her,
it would be a cliché—
but love is made of clichés,
of soft whispers,
of cringy laughter,
of moments that hold too much meaning.
and she's here,
on my birthday,
and all I need is her.

Entry 5: 18/09/2023

I sit alone,
in an unknown city,
with a single candle on a cupcake,
and no one to blow it out with me.
She left,
and the path back to her
was erased with time.

The throne we built together
now empty,

lies vacant in wait,
and the world around it crumbles
and fades.
our castle of love—
dust and echoes,
a kingdom of what-ifs.
and things planned
that never came to be.

And I am forgetting.
Forgetting the scent of her hair,
or the tones of her voice,
or how she pronounced my name,
or how she would flirt and smile.
I am forgetting the little things that made us,
the smaller details of love,
and every day I do a little more,
and a little more,
and a little more,
and a little more,
more of me,
more of happiness,
more of life.

Entry 6: 10/12/2023

I think I'm falling in love.

Loneliness

If you ask me on a regular day,
I will tell you that I am happy.
And I wouldn't be lying—
I am happy.
Happier than ever.
I've been finding my peace,
the one I lost long ago,
finding my place,
that was long forgotten.

But then there are days.
Days like today,
when it all seems to come crashing down,
when the weight of silence
feels louder than the world.
Everyone speaks of love,
of loss,
of pain,
of heartbreak.

The sheer loneliness of being around people
and feeling alone.
Of hoping someone notices.
Of hoping that there is one shred of hope and light
that comes your way on nights like this,
when you feel nothing.

Absolutely nothing.

And nothing
wants to pull you out of it.
Nothing
wants to be okay.

But still—
you survive.
You go on.

The sheer loneliness.
It's often not talked about.
And it's so heartbreaking.

alone, all over again.

Tick tock
Tick tock,
and time goes by,
and I sit here, alone,
all over again,
trying to make this rhyme.

Loneliness has always surrounded me
even in rooms with people around,
and there are times
when I feel
all I am,
is a scream,
and an empty sound.

My life often feels
like a one-way glass,
where I see them
and feel their echoes ring.
Yet, I am invivisble,

and undone,
uncertain,
and unheard.

I don't know why I do this,
why I spill these words into silence.
Maybe it's a cry for help.
Maybe it's just the truth.
All I know is—
I am alone,
all over again,
and there is no end in sight.